Omagh - The Past in Postcards

Omagh has existed a lot longer than both photography and postcards. The images here are 120 years old at most and while many of the street features appear to remain the same there have been many subtle changes over the years. Postcards allow us to explore a past that our ancestors would have been familiar with. Postcards also provide a visual resource for aspects of the past, which may not always have been written down.

Postcards were a cheap and effective means of communication, well within the reach of the master and servant alike. Postcards in their original form existed from the 1870s but they were simple buff cards with an impressed stamp. The idea was that they would contain information only and would be carried for less than the letter rate. As imaginative people began to draw and print designs on cards, the debate about what was a 'Postcard' began. The deciding body was the General Post Office who set out and enforced the postal regulations. It was, put simply, a matter of revenue. If a card contained anything other than information then the Post Office wanted the letter rate for it. Even when the regulations were relaxed you could only put the address on the back, so people began writing on the front. In 1903 the regulations were relaxed further and cards were divided on the back for address and message. A whole new market opened up and it was not long before publishers of photographs and prints entered the market, using images they already had before commissioning photographers to take new images.

From around 1905 people began to collect picture postcards, putting them in albums or stuffing them in drawers. They did so for a variety of reasons, some because it was a new craze, some because they wished to preserve messages from friends or family and some because they liked the images.

Friends and relatives added to the collection of a loved one, even if they did not collect for themselves.

Cards were sold, given away free in novels or magazines and used as advertising for shops or products. They were produced in their thousands, hundreds, tens and singularly.   What has survived is only a fraction of what was produced, but it runs into millions. Many cards have no worth but others, because they have been produced in small numbers or have historic significance, have a value.

My collection is primarily of Omagh and this is what will be shown in my book. I like the fact that the cards have been sought out and treasured before. Perhaps they have lain abroad, unloved, until the Internet has given them the opportunity to come home.

This is one way for me to share my passion for Omagh postcards with others. Although I will provide as much guidance as I can, the images are the main thing; they can evoke the past in a way that words often cannot. I hope you enjoy looking at these images as much as I enjoy collecting them.

Martin Taggart

High Street

Omagh, Augt 17 1902

All well –

A very early view of High Street probably dating from around 1895. These cards were printed on white card and some are more discoloured than others. In 1902 you could only put the address on the back so messages were often put on the front.

Omagh, 24th Oct 1904

Dear C/ will Jon ~ some of
the others come up tomorrow
(Tuesday)? — come early
and Jon know Jon can
stay late, there is beautiful
moon-light. Got home alright
last Tuesday, Lou to all, in haste
Yours L—

Drumragh Church

Another in this early series posted in 1904, it would have been issued in 1901/1902 from an earlier photo. At this time the publishers would have been using existing photos rather than taking new ones. Drumragh Church would have been a familiar landmark.

6

Omagh, _May 8th_ 190 3

The Convent

Many Thanks for parcel safely received yesterday afternoon, very nice useful things. Will write when I hear again from you. Leaving home Tues for a couple of weeks at seaside. _yes ever._ _J.J.E.M.Brown_

This third card in the series shows the Convent and as you can see was posted in 1903. There would have been six cards in the set and I have no idea what the other cards might have been.

7

Court House. Omagh.

The Courthouse in about 1895. Not a postcard but a photograph. The caption accompanied the photograph when I bought it. The railings and the clock are the most distinctive features.

This series of cards is called the Reliable Series and was produced by Walter Richie and Sons of Edinburgh. It is likely that the cards were sold mainly in Connell's stationery shop in High Street, with later cards being produced under the shop's name.

Photographers would use this format when the view would not fit into the landscape mode. The scene was probably set up in the sense that the photographer surely asked the two young schoolboys to stop in the foreground. The cart coming down the hill is likely happenstance but the photographer would have waited for something of interest to include in the scene.

Quigley's Coach works is listed as being in Kevlin Road and it is likely that the front of the premises was. The business survived up until the 1930s when it was shown as being in John Street and it sold motor vehicles instead of making coaches.

JAMES STREET AND CHURCH STREET, OMAGH.

9

High Street, Omagh.

Another familiar image of Omagh. The one steeple of the Sacred Heart helps to date it to before 1900. As you will see from other views of High Street, if the second steeple had been built it would have been visible from this angle.

High Street, Omagh

The same view but coloured. Note that Miss Connell's shop is no longer in shot but we can see more clearly the scaffold around the church steeple. Of course this is not exactly the colour of the town, someone who had not seen the town would have coloured this.

Omagh.

RELIABLE SERIES

A card from the same series, not in the best of condition but it does point to a bygone age in more ways than one. The postmark on the front is not that unusual; it is clear and legible. It shows that postcards were taken from town to town and that the Post Office opened early.

Omagh from Court House.

This view of Omagh is unusual in that it has been taken from the Court House. The camera is on the upper level if not on the roof itself. It is likely that although the postcard dates from around 1904/05 that the image itself was taken pre 1900.

1st Presbyterian Church Omagh

An early view of the 1st Presbyterian Church on the Dublin Road. This view does not show the walls and railings so most likely it was taken from inside the gates.

14

Leap Bridge, Omagh.

RELIABLE WR&S SERIES.

The same publisher but a slightly different format. It is likely that there were two versions of each scene, the full frame and this faded edge series.

Market Street, Omagh.

RELIABLE WR &C SERIES.

Market Street before the turn of the 20th Century. This version of the card is common enough; the street is busy with people and activity. I particularly like the every day scene with the man up the ladder in the background.

16

Waterfall, Lover's Retreat, Omagh.

RELIABLE WH&S SERIES.

There are so many cards of public beauty spots that it is often difficult to be sure if they are already in my collection or not. The same view may have been passed on from publisher to publisher.

Lover's Retreat, Omagh.

RELIABLE [WR S S] SERIES.

When I bought this card recently I was not sure if I already had it but since it was part of the early Reliable series I took a chance. As I collect any postcards to do with Omagh I find that even if I already have the card it may be different in some small way.

Omagh from Courthouse.

This vignette view of 'Omagh From Courthouse' does not record a publisher but it is without doubt a Reliable card. It is obviously from an early series as the back is not divided for address and message. This card illustrates how much information can be lost using this format.

Leap Bridge and Mill, Omagh.

RELIABLE [WR&S] SERIES

An early scene of the Leap Bridge and Mill Omagh. The card was posted in 1910 but the photo would have been taken around 1900, if not before. This series would have been published time and time again. The card was posted in Newtownstewart to Victoria Bridge.

20

A postcard showing a train at Omagh Railway Station. There is no dating evidence but I would guess the 1930s or 1940s. A note on the back says that the train was built in 1912. I have yet to see a card showing the Railway Station in detail.

This card shows the turntable at Omagh Railway station. There does not seem to be an engine attached to the goods wagon. In the area behind the turntable there appears to be vegetable patches under cultivation.

High Street, and Court House, Omagh.

A Military Band and some type of ceremony in front of the Court House some time in 1903 or early 1904. The Inniskillen Memorial, not present here, was erected in November 1904. Also, McCadin's shop was taken over by Blacks some time in 1904.

23

High Street, Omagh.

A card from about 1905. The Inniskillen Memorial is in place and Black's shop is open. Below Blacks is Patrick O'Kane's shop. I am not sure what kind of shop it was. There appears to be goods on the pavement further up the street.

24

Dating from around 1905 this scene shows the Court House and the Post Office. The Post Office is the building above Blacks. The Mullin Memorial looks more ornate than in later photos and begs the question, was it cut down before its final demise?

Post Office and Court House, Omagh

A card from about the same time as the previous two, about 1905. This card is titled 'Post Office and Court House'. In truth the view of the Post Office is no clearer here than in the others of High Street and the Court House.

Post Office and Court House, Omagh.

A similar card from the early 1920s. In this case the Post Office is even more obscured by traffic than the earlier card. There is plenty of activity in this scene. The street remains much the same; it is the transport and fashion which is changing.

POST OFFICE AND COURTHOUSE, OMAGH.

A coloured view from the early 1920s. Less activity than the previous card but perhaps it was taken early in the day. There is no way of telling from the clock on the Court House.

COURTHOUSE, OMAGH

A colourful view of the Court House probably taken in the mid 1920s. The Mullin Memorial is still present. As a photograph it is well balanced, the Court House dominates but has to compete with the Inniskillen Memorial and the pedestrians for our full attention.

Court House, Omagh.

This is the real photographic view of the same scene. The negative of this image would have been used to produce the coloured view. My own preference would be for the coloured view. I know it is not exactly true to life but it seems to add something to the scene.

COURT HOUSE, OMAGH.

A view up High Street of the Court House. The card dates from the 1930s but it is difficult to say just when. HZ replaced the JI registration in the photo in the 1940s but cars did not sell quickly in those days and many people had the same car for years and years.

THE COURT HOUSE, OMAGH

A real photographic version of the same card. There is not a lot of extra detail in this version but the sepia tone does give a little extra punch to the scene. The cyclist coming down the hill is sharp.

THE COURT HOUSE, OMAGH

Another real photographic view from the 1930s. Apart from the cars there are a few things to note. One is the lack of railings around the Court House and another is the telephone box to the left of the steps.

COURT HOUSE, OMAGH.

A view from the 1930s again. I find it interesting to look at pictures taken around the same time; they give a real sense of life in the town. People out and about, running messages in their cars, some on official business and some on their own account.

HIGH STREET AND COURTHOUSE, OMAGH   R 5229

A later view, which shows how busy the town was becoming. Just below the Inniskillen Memorial we can see a Scott's Mill lorry parked. There is no entry to the left of the Statue but the street is congested with cars parked without any real order.

HIGH STREET AND COURTHOUSE, OMAGH

R 5229

Another version of the same card. On the right hand side is the Munster and Leinster Bank and the Melville Hotel. It is not possible to see any of the shops at the mouth of Georges Street.

Courthouse, Omagh. 1314.

A view from the late 1930s or the 1940s. The lorry to the right appears to be an army vehicle. The group of people on the steps is interesting in that they appear to be waiting for something to be announced. A Union Flag flies above the building so there may have been a Court in session.

High Street and Courthouse, Omagh.

I have seen so many of these scenes and have bought quite a few of them. This one is interesting because of the banner, which is hanging from the building on the left. Unfortunately, that part of the image is not sharp but there appears to be "Thompsons" and a star on the banner.

This is probably the most common view of Market Street dating from around 1905. The card turns up both in this coloured version and more commonly in the sepia print version. It shows the street well before houses were removed for the new Bridge.

Market Street, Omagh

This is a black and white version of the same scene. It is not exactly the same since it has been slightly reframed and we lose the chimney pots. Sometimes the black and white version makes it easier to read the shop names and see details that the colourist has obscured.

Market Street, Omagh.

An early view of Market Street, not much different from the previous cards. Taken from a very similar position as the other cards. On the left we have a tobacconist but there is very little to tell us the name of the trader. The card dates from the 1920s to 1930s.

MARKET STREET OMAGH.

Taken around the same time as the other cards this street scene has a little more life about it. It has been taken from a similar position to the previous cards. The colours are similar but not quite the same.

Market Street, Omagh.

This real photographic card dates from the nineteen twenties. On the left is Bennetts shop, on the right is Love's Manchester House and below that is Boyers shop. The street is busy but there is very little vehicular traffic. Over leaf is the coloured version of this card.

Market Street, Omagh.

The coloured version is a little brighter but it is not as easy to read the shop names. The dog walking across the street appears happy to wander along on his own, no sign of the owner either side of the street.

MARKET STREET, OMAGH.

Yet another view looking down Market Street. It dates from the late 1930s to the early 1940s. Note the petrol pumps on the left hand side and the girl struggling with the bicycle on the right. These are snapshots in the life of the town.

Market Street, Omagh.

Market Street, looking back up the street. This card dates from the 1920s and is a typical scene of town life. JI 3808 is coming down the hill; men stand on the corner looking towards the camera. There is a barbers shop a little way up the street on the right and a post box on the left.

46

HOUSE FURNISHERS

MARKET STREET, OMAGH

R 5227

A slightly later view of the same junction. On the left we have J B Anderson House Furnishers and Anderson Brothers on the right. This view is much altered today, I think that Anderson Brothers may have been one of the shops demolished to make way for Drumagh Avenue.

47

MARKET STREET, OMAGH.

R.2993.

A clear view of the lower part of Market Street before the new road. On the left we have F A Wellworth and Co Ltd. Not to be confused with F W Woolworth but I doubt if the similarity in names was a coincidence. Wellworth's van is parked on the left, outside the shop.

Market Street, Omagh 1350

This coloured card of Market Street shows the same van on the right hand side as the previous card. The street is alive with activity and the vibrant yellow colour makes the scene stand out. The man crossing the road watches the photographer and not the oncoming car.

Market Street, Omagh

A real photographic card which shows a less busy scene. The photographer is shooting with the sun behind him and as a consequence his shadow is in shot. On the right hand side is the Pretoria Café, other details are slightly bleached by the sun.

Dublin Road and First Presbyterian Church, Omagh

The titles of cards often include Churches in the background. In this case the main interest lies in the Dublin Road and the Church is of secondary interest. On the left hand side we have the Ulster Hall. The card is crudely coloured but is the only card of the Dublin Road I have seen.

I have extracted two elements of this card to allow a better view of Stopes Hotel and the First Presbyterian Church. The old ruin is interesting as it is not possible to see what kind of building it might have been.

Market Street from Campsie Bridge, Omagh. 1352

A card showing Campsie Bridge looking back towards the town. The card dates from the late 1940s to the early 1950s and shows a view of Omagh much altered today. I have walked down this road on many occasions but I don't remember this view.

Market Street from Campsie Bridge, Omagh. 1352

This is a sepia version of the same scene. I am not sure which would have been available first; I suspect that it would have been the colour card to get the most sales and then the printed cards. The colour version is cropped tighter for printing but is essentially the same shot.

An early view of Campsie showing Peter McAleer's Public House on the left. The name still remains but it is now in other ownership; still it is a link with the past. The pub dates from the 1890s. The street scene shows little activity.

Omagh.

This is a black and white version of the same scene. On the right hand side you can see the recess for the Bank of Ireland. The street is almost empty and I have not seen many views of Campsie other than the ones in my collection but there must be at least a few more out there.

56

BRITISH LEGION HUT, OMAGH.

The British Legion Hut in Campsie with the Trophy Gun outside. The Gun arrived in 1923 and this photo would have been taken not long after. I assume that the two men are committee members who were available to pose for the photo.

British Legion Hut, Omagh.

OUR GLORIOUS DEAD

This view dates from the 1940s, judging by the postman's uniform and the War Memorial. The Trophy Gun is still in place at this stage and I am not sure when it was disposed of. When the gun arrived in 1923 it was estimated to be worth £5 to £10 in scrap.

War Memorial, Omagh.

A view of the War Memorial in Omagh. It was unveiled on 28th September 1927 by the Duke of Abercorn. It is the County Tyrone War Memorial commemorating the two thousand men from Tyrone who lost their lives in the Great War.

WAR MEMORIAL, OMAGH

A wider view of the War Memorial. It does not look the same today and is not in its original place. The granite obelisk set on the three steps remains but the surrounding wall and railings are no more. Unlike other WW1 memorials there is no soldier represented.

The Monument to the Royal Inniskillen Fusiliers stood just below the Court House for sixty years. It now stands on Drumragh Avenue having been moved there when the new bridge was opened in 1964.

The Monument was not the first choice as a means of remembering the soldiers who died in the Boer War but it was eventually chosen as a fitting tribute. It had been suggested that a cross should be erected near the railway station. That simple memorial was not followed through and there was some frustration in the town that it was taking so long to erect a monument since Enniskillen had already put up theirs.

In November 1904 the long wait was over and the statue was unveiled on one of the worst days for weather that Omagh had seen in recent years.

The Monument was moved because of traffic problems but in reality its removal did not change a lot, for the better that is.

ROYAL INN. FUS. MONUMENT, OMAGH.

A view of the Monument with a young boy posing beside it. Photographers often liked to place a person in the foreground to give a sense of scale. We can see part of the Mullin Memorial.

Royal Irish Fusiliers Monument, Omagh

62

Royal Inniskilling Fusiliers' Monument, Omagh

53725

JV

This is the coloured view of the Monument card. There is no real variation in this card except for the colour. The clouds and the sky often look the same in colour cards because they were stock images.

The angle of this view has changed and we can see both spires of the Sacred Heart and a clear view of the old Police Station. Produced for Connell Stationer Omagh, the view is slightly different than others.

64

Monument to
The Inniskilling Fusiliers, Omagh.

Connell, Stationer,
Omagh.

ROYAL INNISKILLING FUSILIER MONUMENT, OMAGH.

An interesting card in the series that shows a delivery sitting outside the Court House. The clock says ten to eight, so presumably it is in the morning. A military man is coming down Georges Street.

This is the funeral of Major General Sir Harry Nevile Thompson who was buried in Omagh in June 1925. The card shows the military band and the extent of the funeral procession as it wends its way up from Market Street.

Military Barracks, Omagh.

A view of the Military Barracks in Omagh. The Royal Inniskillen Fusiliers were based in Omagh and were at one time an integral part of the social scene in Omagh. Many Omagh men joined the British Army and served in the Boer War and WW1. Note the two soldiers on the left hand side.

This is the Military Band and soldiers presenting arms at the Court House pre 1904. It is hard to determine what might have been the occasion, perhaps the opening of a Court Session. Although the fact is that the Court House was used for many social events in the past.

Orange Hall, Omagh

A coloured view of the Orange Hall on the Mountjoy Road. The Hall dates from 1869 and was referred to as the 'Protestant Hall'. You can just make out the name plaque for 'Carlisle Villas'. The name of the Yard at the rear of the Hall is not easy to read because of the railings.

69

This is a section of the card showing three circular plaques and a rectangular plaque depicting William Prince of Orange on horseback. The central plaque is of H Cooke, who opened the new Trinity Church in 1856. The outside two are Sir J M Stewart and Capt. M Stewart G.M.

Omagh Shamrocks 1926-27

Back Row (l. to r.): The late H. Bradley, R. Shannon, T. Fiddis, the late J. Mullan, the late J. McFadden, F. Cuthbertson, D. Donnelly (now resident in Canada) and F. Nixon.

Front Row (l. to r.): H. Bradley, P. Rodgers, H. Hackett, J. Reilly, H. Cassidy, the late J. Wilkinson, P. Gilleece and L. McFadden.

A team photo of Omagh Shamrocks from the 1926–27 season. They were not the same Shamrocks who played before the First World War; their strip had large shamrocks on it, similar to the ones the little boys wear here.

This is a photo of Omagh Military FC (1919-1920) more commonly known as 'The Depot' and affectionately known as 'The Skins'. They were the mainstay of the local soccer scene for many years at a time when the local camp was a part of Omagh society at all levels.

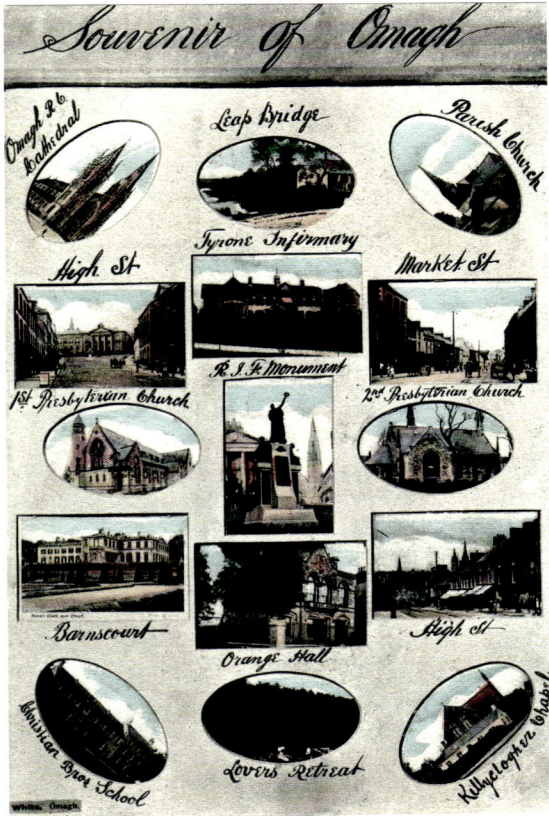

Souvenir of Omagh

Omagh R.C. Cathedral · Leap Bridge · Parish Church · High St · Tyrone Infirmary · Market St · 1st Presbyterian Church · R.I.C. Monument · 2nd Presbyterian Church · Barnscourt · Orange Hall · High St · Christian Bros School · Lovers Retreat · Killyclogher Chapel

Christian Bros School

Killyclogher Chapel

Orange Hall

A multi-view card with fifteen scenes produced by or for Whites of Omagh. The card shows many familiar scenes but there are at least three cards from this series that I do not have. The Orange Hall scene is different from the cards I have and I do not have cards of the other two.

Omagh from N.

Old Mill, Leap Bridge, Omagh

Market Street, Omagh

OMAGH

Post Office and Court House, Omagh

A classic example of how publishers recycled images, here are four fairly common views of the town and surrounds to which a crest has been added. It is quite common to see heraldic coats of arms on cards.

74

COURTHOUSE.

RIVER & R.C. CHURCH.

HIGH STREET.

OMAGH

OMAGH.

R.3387

JAMES STREET & PARISH CHURCH.

This is a multi-view card showing three cards that I have yet to come across. I have the Courthouse and High Street cards but not the other three scenes. The James Street card is interesting as it shows a partial view of John Street with Weir & McFarland on the corner.

HIGH STREET

RIVER AND R.C. CHURCH

AERIAL VIEW

OMAGH

THE GORTIN GLEN

MARKET STREET   R.4842

A multi-view card, which contains many familiar scenes. Sometimes the cards contain the standard cards already published and sometimes there are small differences in detail, which suggests it may be another card or a different negative at least.

Leap Mill.

Lissen Bridge.

Court House.

OMAGH

Lovers' Retreat

Crevenagh Bridge.

This multi-view card shows a view of Leap Mill I have not seen before. There is a figure of a man on the right and a woman in the centre. The other interesting shot is that of the Lissen Bridge. There are a number of Omagh bridges which I have yet to see on a postcard.

This is the central image of a damaged card I bought some time ago. The damaged part showed the details of the Royal Arms Hotel. John Porter ran the Reform Stores as well as the Arms. This was an advertising card for the Royal Arms Hotel and dates from the early 1900s.

GEORGES STREET, OMAGH

Georges Street in the early 1920s. The card was produced for Gorman's shop on the right, which probably explains why the photographer chose to concentrate on getting the shop in shot, rather than including the spires of the Sacred Heart.

George Street, Omagh

Another card of Georges Street, earlier than the first and this time the photographer has taken a portrait shot to make sure that the spires and crosses are included. Note the street is named as 'George Street'.

80

An early view looking down High Street. The White Hart Hotel is on the right hand side and the White Hart sign is clearly visible. The coach belongs to the Hotel and would have been used to bring guests from and to the Railway Station.

High Street from Court House, Omagh.

A view dating from the early 1920s showing the Mullin Memorial Water Fountain. There were frequent debates about the condition of the fountain and it was suggested that the Inniskillen Memorial would be moved up the street to replace it. Note the man at the Bank window.

High Street (from Court House) Omagh.

A coloured card from the late 1920s or early 1930s. The Ulster Bank is on the left hand side having moved from the site of the Town Hall some years previously. The publisher is not recorded but there is a series of cards similarly coloured.

High Street, Omagh.

A real photographic card dating from the 1920s/30s. The one thing it illustrates is that not all photographic cards are equal in quality. In this case the image is not sharp enough to identify much detail.

High Street, Omagh. 1345.

A printed card from a few years later. Although this was well before the Inniskillen Memorial was moved, it already shows how casual parking was beginning to cause problems. In my opinion the solution was not to move the Monument, other towns managed after all.

HIGH STREET FROM COURTHOUSE, OMAGH.

A heavily coloured card from the 1920s or early 1930s. The street lamp that once illuminated the Mullin Fountain is in place but the Fountain appears to be removed at this point. Of course the Inniskillen Monument was never painted green.

86

HIGH STREET, OMAGH.

R.3008.

Probably taken in the late 1940s or early 1950s this scene is very similar to the previous ones. The interest lies in the two small boys who appear to be collecting car numbers. Note the car parked tight to the Monument, a habit more common years before. There are parking bays on the right.

HIGH STREET, OMAGH, CO. TYRONE

R 6265

A view of High Street showing the Post Office where the Old White Hart Hotel was. The modern building is out of sync with the rest of the street but that is progress for you. The Council had previously tried to move the Monument and a few years after this photo was taken, they succeeded.

HIGH STREET, OMAGH, CO. TYRONE

R 5873

A clear view of the Ulster Bank looking down High Street. This is a real photographic card that gives an overall impression of the street, rather than any detail of shops and buildings other than the Ulster Bank.

HIGH STREET, OMAGH, CO. TYRONE

A real photographic card of High Street, not a great deal of detail here but the one thing of interest is the handcart parked against the Monument. I find there is always something in every card that gives a glimpse of life in the town.

90

This view dates from about 1905, the Hospital being built around 1899. The original Omagh Infirmary was in Main Street (High Street/Market Street) and was a substantial building. This Hospital was designed to serve a wider area than Omagh itself.

TYRONE INFIRMARY.

A closer view without the cows or the fields in shot. The area around the Hospital is now car parking or housing, this card shows what it was like around 1907. Note the open window top left; people spent a lot of time watching photographers.

Tyrone Infirmary, Omagh

Another printed view, which shows the Hospital from the town side. It shows the young trees, which would have been planted just after the Hospital was completed.

Tyrone Infirmary.

A view from the other side; and maybe a little later, as many of the trees seem to be growing up. The road in front of the Hospital seems more like a lane than the busy road it is today.

Tyrone Hospital, Omagh.

A real photographic view from the 1920s or 1930s. An ambulance sits at the front door along with the car with the JI registration. There appears to have been more built to the side of the main building. Also the name is changing, with the Infirmary falling from use.

TYRONE COUNTY HOSPITAL. OMAGH.

Another real photographic card, which has lost a little detail with the photographer shooting in strong sunlight. Nurses look out from the nearest window and the name has become the Tyrone County Hospital. It may be before or after the previous card, it is hard to tell.

Tyrone Infirmary, Omagh.

A coloured card which shows the front of the Hospital some time in the 1920s. Although there is little dating evidence, the style of the card would suggest it is before 1930.

THE COUNTY HOSPITAL, OMAGH

R 6045

An enlarged Hospital from the late 1950s or early 1960s. Many of the details are clearer in this photo than in others. The title reflects what it was called locally, 'The County'.

I bought this card because it has a reference to Omagh on the back. The Nursing Sister suggests that it was taken at a Hospital and the large group of men suggests that it is the Tyrone and Fermanagh Hospital, but that is just conjecture on my part.

KNOCK -NA- MOE CASTLE, OMAGH

Unfortunately Knock na Moe is no more but at one time it was the home of the Stack family and later became an hotel. In 1959 when the Court House was being renovated it was used for the court sessions. US troops were stationed here in WW2 so it had quite a history. This is an early card.

A superb aerial view of Omagh showing four of the churches. We have Trinity, The Methodist Church, St Columba's Parish Church and the Sacred Heart in view. The Fair Green and John Street are in view as well as Gallows Hill.

AERIAL VIEW, OMAGH

R 4491

Another aerial view taken from more to the right. We have a clearer view of the Methodist Church but we can only see the edge of Trinity. There is a clear view of Sedan Avenue with the river running along side.

The Three Churches, Omagh

Down to the ground and we see three of the churches from about 1905 or so. I have not seen a separate card of the Methodist Church but I am sure they must exist, after all there are plenty of both St Columba's and the Sacred Heart.

The Three Churches, Omagh

This is the real photographic card of the same scene. On the left of Church Street runs the premises of Quigley's coach works and it is very likely that the cart sitting at the top of the street is one ready for collection.

104

Second Presbyterian Church, Omagh

Trinity Presbyterian Church is said to be the oldest church in Omagh. As a boy I passed this church on a daily basis. I often stopped to look at it; I have always liked churches. Here it is described as the Second Presbyterian, the First Presbyterian being on the Dublin Road.

Trinity Church, Omagh

A black and white view of the same church. This time it is referred to as Trinity Church, which is what I had always heard it called. I note that the church was listed in 1910 as being in John Street. In the mid 1800s it was described as being on the Dromore Road.

This view of Trinity Church is slightly elevated to look over the railings. The card is later, dating from the 1930s or 1940s based on the electricity cables and the fact that the tree at the front has matured.

Lislimnaghan

Moving slightly outside the town, this is Lislimnaghan Church of Ireland near Mountjoy. It has changed little over the years. The Church celebrates its 150th anniversary this year (2012).

First Presbyterian Church, Omagh

The First Presbyterian Church on the Dublin Road. There are a number of these cards which have been altered slightly by the publisher in both detail and colour. This was done to give the impression that they are different cards where in fact they are all from the same negative.

First Presbyterian Church, Omagh

The same scene again but coloured differently. There is a lump where the dog was but it doesn't look like the original dog. On the left hand side we have part of a lamppost, which is not in the original scene.

First Omagh Presbyterian Church.

A similar scene from around the same time but with no people. The lamppost is fully in view this time and the colours have a warm glow as if the photo was taken at sunset. The truth is that artists looking at black and white negatives created these effects.

1st Omagh Presbyterian Church.

A view from a later period, probably the 1920s. There are wires in the background and I assume that they are electricity wires. There is little change in the overall composition of the scene; the colours are no more realistic but they create a pleasant, idealised view.

A drawing of Omagh Sacred Heart Church, which was completed in 1899. The Church replaced the old St Peter & St Paul Chapel in Brook Street. Neither was the parish Church, that honour remains with St Mary's Drumragh after which the parish is named.

Although the Sacred Heart is impressive, it was never a Cathedral as referenced in this card.

It was built at a time when there was a new found confidence in Omagh. For example there had been several attempts to establish a broadly nationalist newspaper in Omagh but within a few years of the building of this Church the Ulster Herald established itself as a viable alternative to the Tyrone Constitution, which had existed from 1844.

Over the page is a similar card, which describes it as the New Church, Omagh.

Omagh Cathedral.

The New Church, Church Street, Omagh.

THE SACRED HEART CHURCH, OMAGH

A real photographic card of the Sacred Heart Church taken from the rear. It was probably taken from the schoolyard of the Christian Brothers School. It is not the sharpest of photos and the photographer or printer has cut off the tops of the steeples.

Sacred Heart Church. Omagh.

A close up view of the front of the Sacred Heart. There is no publisher given but it is unlikely to be the same publisher as the previous card. The card shows some detail of the architecture of the church, but it could be sharper.

INTERIOR OF R.C. CHURCH, OMAGH   R 4612

A real photographic card of the interior of the Sacred Heart Church. It is dark but still gives some idea of the size of the Church.

A card of Castle Street, which concentrates on the Church. There is what appears to be a public house part way up on the right hand side but otherwise there is very little detail of the street itself.

R. C. Church from N., Omagh

Church of the Sacred Heart, Omagh

A view of Church Street and the Sacred Heart Church. Note the buildings both sides of the Church. The woman going into her house but lingering to watch and the other figure add scale to the image.

A real photographic card of the same street some years later. The houses below the church seem to have gone by this stage. There are no people to give it scale but the car on the left hand side does that.

R. 3014

R.C. CHURCH, OMAGH

FZ 5357

Parish Church, Omagh

53737

A view of St Columba's Church of Ireland described here as the Parish Church. This is an early coloured card dating from around 1905 but the image itself could well be older.

121

A real photographic card of the same Church. It is later than the first card because of the electricity wires. The photographer has cut off the spire in an effort to get a closer view of the front of the Church.

122

ST. COLUMBA'S PARISH CHURCH, OMAGH

The Loreto Nuns came to Omagh in 1855 and were initially housed in Georges Street until the present Convent was completed in 1859. The dates on this first set of cards range from before WW1 up to the 1930s. They reveal the daily life of the Nuns and pupils both within the Convent and school.

There is no publisher recorded on the cards and from the limited number I have seen they appear to have been sent by pupils at the school. It may be that the cards were not available commercially within the town but were produced for the Convent itself for use by the staff and pupils. Many other cards of the Convent were produced for sale in the town.

This card is a simple scene of the statue of Our Lady in front of the Convent but it also shows the greenhouse with a Nun observing the photographer.

The Loreto Convent, Omagh   Our Lady

The Loreto Convent, Omagh   National School

A wide view within the grounds showing the National School. I spent my first year of school here before moving on to the Christian Brothers. I remember that we were envious of the boys who were allowed to play in the sandpit.

The Loreto Convent, Omagh — Side View

Part of the same series and posted in 1915 this card shows a side view of the Convent. There is a male figure in the background, probably the grounds man. This is a more intimate portrait of the Convent than others, obviously a competent photographer.

The Loreto Convent, Omagh

Parlour

This card is titled 'Parlour' but it is essentially music practice. Although the room appears to look well decorated, it is functional rather than opulent. The bare floorboards show that function rather than decoration was more important within the Convent.

Loreto Convent, Omagh   Laboratory

A wonderful glimpse of education pre WW1. The card is titled 'Laboratory' and that is just what it was; a science class in progress. The Nun sits at the top of the table and the girls work away. It may well have been set up for the photo but it would be representative of the time.

Convent Omagh.

A picturesque view of the Convent with two Nuns standing at the front door looking down towards the camera. It may suggest that the photographer did not ask permission. The card dates from the 1930s and was not sent through the post.

The Chapel, Loreto Convent, Omagh.

This looks like the same style of postcard except that unlike the rest of the series it has a border around it. It shows the Convent Chapel and on the next page is a full-length view of the Nuns at prayer.

The Loreto Convent, Omagh

Chapel

Convent and R.C. Church, Omagh

A very common card of the Convent and Sacred Heart Church but you can also see the steeple of St Columba's Parish Church. The card has been coloured and as you will see over leaf in the same scene the colours did not always remain the same.

131

CONVENT AND R.C. CHURCH, OMAGH.

This vignette card has been produced to take advantage of views the publisher already had. This was a way of making the card look fresh and new. The colours are not exactly the same but that was probably a deliberate attempt to make the card look different.

Loretto Convent, Omagh.

When a photographer could not put a person in the foreground he would include an animal to give the picture perspective. After all he could easily have walked up to the little gate and taken the photo from there. It reminds us that there were still farms within the town boundaries in 1905.

Loret Convent, Omagh

The view is fairly standard, with the steeple of St Columba's Parish Church in the background. It dates from the 1930s and the unusual thing is the spelling of 'Loreto'. It is usual enough to see it spelt with two 'T's but without the 'O' it is very strange indeed.

The Convent, Omagh

RELIABLE SERIES 832

Essentially the same scene as the last card but completely different colours. These cards would have been typeset and coloured in Germany. Once they had the master copy these cards would have been printed from it. Of course any mistakes would remain but none here.

THE LORETO CONVENT. OMAGH

A real photographic view of the Convent. Many of these real photographic cards are difficult to date and you often have to go on style and process. I would say that this is sometime in the 1930s but there is nothing to date it precisely.

Front Avenue, Loreto Convent, Omagh.

A card showing the front avenue leading up to the Convent. The card dates from the 1930s and was posted during the Second World War. There is no publisher recorded but as with other similar black and white cards it appears to have been used by a pupil.

Technical Schools, Omagh. 965.

This is a card of the Technical Schools Omagh. There are pupils in shot but there is little other detail. The Technical School was co-located with the Academy in Omagh. There was a pedestrian entrance in Johnston Park but the main way in was by the Dublin Road.

Loughmuck, Omagh

A view of the road along-side the Lough. It is likely that this is the trap which brought the photographer from the town. The card dates from about 1905.

LOUGHMUCK OMAGH.

The same narrow road but this time we see cattle being taken for water in the Lough. The name Lough Muck would suggest that the area was associated with pigs at some time.

Loughend, Loughmuck, Omagh

A very picturesque scene at Lough Muck. The card dates from about 1905 and the boat nearest us has been left uncoloured.

Lough-end, Loughmuck, Omagh

Essentially the same scene but an elaborate border has been added, showing shamrocks and a harp. Again this was a way for a publisher to get a little more from a card. In some cases they would sell their images off to other publishers or produce cards for local shops.

BESIDE LOUGH MUCK, NEAR OMAGH, CO. TYRONE   R 5231

Lough Muck in a real photographic card. The card is nice enough but there is little about it, other than the caption to show that it is Lough Muck.

LOUGH MUCK, OMAGH.

This view of Lough Muck shows a wide view of the Lough. It probably dates from the 1930s as we can see the swimming platform at the far side of the Lough. It also shows the farming land around the Lough.

BATHING AT LOUGH MUCK, OMAGH.

Lough Muck was the venue for the Omagh Swimming and Life Saving club, which was set up in 1930. This photo would date from that period. It shows the diving platform and the rafts that swimmers would swim to.

Lough Muck, Omagh

A similar view to the last one but this time it is a real photograph and was likely taken at a Swimming Gala. Galas were held in the summer months. This photo shows a section of the crowd, who came as spectators. Judging by the crowd it was a popular day out.

LOUGH END, LOUGHMUCK, OMAGH 53730

Loughend Lough Muck in a real photographic card. It can be difficult to come across the real photographic cards as they were more expensive than the printed ones and often issued in smaller numbers.

THE STRULE BRIDGE, OMAGH

R 6270

A very colourful view of the river, bridge and spires of the Sacred Heart. In recent years this has been a favourite view for photographers. Bell's Bridge as a name for the bridge seems to have come back into use after the new road and bridge were opened in the 1960s.

A real photographic card of Omagh from Cannon Hill. The railway bridge is no longer there and of course the whole area has changed quite significantly. It is rare to get a view from this side of the town.

BELL'S BRIDGE, OMAGH

A view of Bell's Bridge from the left hand side exiting Bridge Street. Early photos of the Bridge from the other side are titled Strule Bridge. This photo captures a popular pastime, fishing, which continues to this day.

150

NEW BRIDGE, OMAGH

A coloured view of Abbey Bridge referred to simply as 'New Bridge'. The metal bridge was eventually replaced because it could not support the weight of the traffic passing over it. Note the people on the bridge keeping an eye on the photographer.

151

Omagh from N.

A view of Abbey Bridge from the opposite side. It shows the Sacred Heart, the spire of St Columba's Church and the Strule River itself. Omagh is a town where three rivers meet but it is not always possible to get good views of the rivers themselves.

Strule Bridge, Omagh

A coloured view of Strule Bridge Omagh. I have never seen a card with the view from this side with the title 'Bell's Bridge'. The bridge got both names and, presumably, was commonly referred to as 'Strule Bridge' as it spanned the Strule. The Shop at the end of Bridge Street is W Calvin.

Strule Bridge, Omagh

Sometimes with photos taken from a similar spot it is difficult to notice the differences but in this card there are a few differences from the last one. For a start there are people on the bridge and the name on the shop in Bridge Street is R Patrick. I suspect this is the later card.

154

ST. RULE'S BRIDGE. OMAGH

This sepia card is mistitled 'St. Rule's Bridge'. Such mistakes happened because the card was probably typeset and printed in Germany. Perhaps the publisher spotted the mistake and only a few cards escaped into the wild, more likely it wasn't noticed until the reprint.

Strule Bridge, Omagh

The correct version of the card but there are slight changes, not least the framing and the positioning of the caption. I say correct version but it could be argued the 'Strule' and 'St. Rule' captions are both incorrect since this is 'Bell's Bridge'.

Crevenagh Bridge, Omagh

Crevenagh Bridge Omagh is of course now more commonly referred to as 'King James Bridge'; names sometimes fall out of favour. It is said that King James crossed the bridge on his way to Derry. In latter years the bridge has had traffic lights installed to deal with modern traffic.

CREVENAGH BRIDGE, OMAGH.

A printed version of the card, which is a little clearer than the real photographic version. This image dates from the 1930s and shows the bridge as it used to be. W. K. Ellis in 'A Hundred Years A-Milling' laments that the council repaired the bridge with "unsightly cement".

These cards are known as mechanical or pull-out cards. They typically contain twelve views of the cards in the series. It was imaginative recycling of views by publishers. In this case these are three views for which I do not have the corresponding postcards.

A large letter greetings card showing the Omagh Crest. Cards such as these would have been produced for lots of towns and were a cheap way for publishers to customise cards for individual places. With only five letters in the name, Omagh was ideal for producing such a card.

Old Gaol & Barracks, Omagh.

Looking across Abbey Bridge is the old Gaol and beyond that St Lucia Barracks. The gaol opened in 1804, the Court House later occupied the previous site, and it closed in 1904. It may well have been closed when this photo was taken. The right hand side of the bridge is not clear. Hoardings?

Old Goal and Barracks, Omagh.

A sepia version of the previous card showing the Abbey Bridge, in the background there is the old Gaol and Army Barracks. Notice the misspelling of 'Gaol'. The puzzle remains as to what is on the right hand side at the end of the bridge.

162

Old Gaol and Barracks, Omagh

Another view of the Abbey Bridge, the old Gaol and Army Barracks. It is more or less the same scene with a border added but the right hand side remains unresolved. It is typical of how the manipulation of images by publishers can lead to distortion and uncertainty.

Fair Green Omagh.

This is the only card of a fair in Omagh I know about. I recently saw an image on the Internet titled 'Fair Day Omagh', except it was actually The Moy. Fair Green was at the back of Trinity Presbyterian Church. There were other markets in the town but I have not seen cards of them.

Drumlegagh Manse, Newtownstewart

I have always kept Drumlegagh cards with my Omagh cards. Just after I was married we rented a bungalow near Drumlegagh. I have always liked this card with the dog in the foreground, obviously not a working dog but a family pet.

Drumlegagh, Newtownstewart

It is rare enough to get postcards of places too small to be villages, which are in fact townlands with farms and a few central buildings. This is Drumlegagh Presbyterian Church but it is not identified as such. It is a pleasant country scene at the beginning of the twentieth century.

There is no caption on this card but it was sent from Edenfel in 1908. Edenfel on the Crevenagh Road was the home of the Buchanan family who were involved with the military and the administration of the town. It is unlikely this card was available commercially.

"EDENFEL"

Another view of Edenfel posted in 1937. The initials of the sender end with a 'B', so it may well have been sent by a member of the Buchanan family. Edenfel was the site of a weather observation station.

Leap Bridge and Mills, Omagh.

A view of the Leap Bridge and Mills near Omagh. The fast flowing Camowen River was excellent for turning mill wheels before the advent of electricity made it possible to place a mill anywhere.

Accept this friendly token,
And 'till we meet again,
'Twill serve to keep unbroken
The links of memory's
chain.

Waterfall at Leap Bridge, Omagh

This card is an example of what publishers did to spruce up a card. The little verses were sentimental and fully intended to be so. Shamrocks, round towers and spinning wheels were added to make the card more enticing to the tourist market.

A picturesque view of the Bridge and Mill. Such cards would have been sent to emigrants to remind them of home. Cards that captured the romance of home were often preferred to more realistic scenes.

171

Leap Bridge, Omagh

RELIABLE SERIES 144

Connell, Stationer, Omagh.

A card from the same series, this time showing the bridge on its own without the mill. Publishers had up to twelve cards in a series, so separate cards of bridges or other features were often used to fill up the series.

Leap Bridge and Mill, Omagh

A real photographic card which shows the millwheel that would have powered the mill. The card dates from the 1930s. Earlier cards date from around 1900 but the wheel is not as visible as it is here.

CAMOWEN RIVER AT LEAP BRIDGE, OMAGH.

A colourful scene, which shows more of the Camowen River than the bridge. Often photographers would place people or objects in the foreground. Here there is just a shot of the river and bridge, not natural in colour but pleasant nevertheless.

LEAP BRIDGE AND MILL, OMAGH.

A printed view of the Mill showing the wheel, for some reason it seems clearer than the real photographic card. This card would date from the 1930s and although not as attractive as some of the coloured cards, it has a certain charm.

Waterfall at Leap Bridge, Omagh

A printed card which shows the waterfall at Leap Bridge. There are houses in the background but it is difficult to locate them precisely. The card is slightly different from others of the Mill.

LEAP BRIDGE, OMAGH, CO. TYRONE.   R.6268

A real photographic card and a close up of the Leap Bridge itself. The circles in the water would suggest that there were fish rising in the river. The Camowen would have been rich in salmon.

THE LEAP BRIDGE, OMAGH

A rare view of the Bridge and Mill from the other side. The card was posted in 1911 but it is probable that the original image dates from around 1905. The border and decoration were most likely added by the publisher to produce a new card from an existing scene.

LEAP MILLS AND WATERFALL
OMAGH.

An early card which gives a more panoramic view of the Mills and their daily operation. Note the figure by the millwheel and the fact that we can see most of the buildings in context. The card has not been posted but it would date from 1905 or thereabouts.

Leap Mills & Waterfall, Omagh.

This is a similar view but the issue of the card is different. The title is in red at the top but apart from this, and the condition of the card, the view is very much the same. It is probably the case that images were exchanged between publishers.

Old Mill, Leap Bridge, Omagh

Yet another view of Leap Bridge. This time the card is titled 'Old Mill Leap Bridge'. We get a clear view of the mill and millwheel but there are no people in the picture. The river is full reminding us that when the three rivers met, Omagh was often overcome with water.

Old Mill, Leap Bridge, Omagh

A vignette view of the Old Mill Leap Bridge. The card shown here would have been reissued in this format to make use of a pre-existing image, giving it a fresh look. The essential elements are present: the Mill and the River Camowen, with Shamrocks added for effect.

The Lovers Retreat has been a beauty spot for many years. This portrait view is unusual as it shows houses in the background. On a card posted in 1907 the sender wrote:

"This is a nice place quite near but none of the photos give a good enough view of it. It is quite large with a river running through and trees."

I have read many things about the area but much is simply confusion. For example I read recently that the area was named after the weeping willows, which made the lovers weep. Fanciful conjecture at best, after all which came first the willows or the Retreat?

No doubt that the secluded Retreat, just a few miles from the centre of Omagh, proved popular with 'Lovers' but the explanation is a little less poetic. The name is a corruption of 'Lodvers Retreat', the original owners of the Retreat. I am not sure when the name change happened but I have one card which shows the original name.

Lovers' Retreat from above the Waterfall, Omagh.

53723 J.V.

A fairly common view of the 'Lover's Retreat'. When to use an apostrophe seemed to be just as much a problem in the past as it is today. The girl on the footbridge and the old lady coming along carrying a basket adds a lot to the scene.

184

An early view of the Waterfall at the Lovers Retreat with three young girls sitting on the rocks. The colouring of the card has left the girl in the white dress poorly defined. The card is not posted so there is no way to date it precisely but it is from about 1905 or before.

Lover's Retreat, Omagh

This is the real photographic version of the card and it was posted in 1905. The detail is clearer although it is essentially the same card. It was only when looking at this card closely that I spotted the young boy on the pathway to the left. He is in the coloured version too.

186

Connell, Stationer, Omagh.

A view of the Waterfall produced for Connell Stationer of High Street. Sometimes the publisher would omit his own details in favour of letting the local shop appear to have produced the card. This is a colourful card but it is not in itself unusual.

Waterfall, Lodver's Retreat, Omagh   Reliable W.R.A.S. Series.

Connell Stationer, Omagh.

On the face of it this is the same card as the previous one but if you look closely you will see that this is titled 'The Lodver's Retreat', which I have always understood to be the original name. The explanation being that the land belonged to a family called 'Lodver'.

A view of the Waterfall described as the Salmon Leap Lover's Retreat. At first I thought there was a person fishing but it is an optical illusion created by the way the light reflects off the trees.

THE WATERFALL AT LOVERS RETREAT. OMAGH.

A very colourful depiction of the Waterfall at the Lovers Retreat. I often visited the Lovers Retreat on warm and even hot summer days but I have never seen the water this blue or the vegetation so green.

High Street Omagh in the early 1920s. It is certainly pre 1929 as the Mullin Memorial Water Fountain is still in place. On the left we see the Royal Arms car, which would have been used to take guests from and to the Railway Station. Note also the Cinema on the left.

High Street, Omagh.

Another view of High Street in the early 1920s. The detail in these real photo cards is excellent but it can depend on the skill of the photographer to capture pin sharp images. The car in the foreground has a JI registration.

High Street, Omagh

A wonderfully animated street scene from the early 1930s. It was taken from just past the Royal Arms Hotel and the Hotel car is in the foreground. Note the cattle further up the street, a good reason for the man with the brush and wheelbarrow to be out on the street.

High Street, Omagh

This is the first postcard of Omagh that I bought. At first I asked all the usual questions: how old is it? Did they have colour photography in the early 1900s? The card dates from about 1905 and an artist has added the colour. This is still one of my favourite views of Omagh.

194

High Street, Omagh.

As the postcard craze took off around 1905/1906, publishers competed to produce new cards of familiar areas. The cards may have only been taken a few months apart but depending on the location of the camera and the angle, the street can look different every time.

This view shows a very busy street scene but if you look closely you will notice that much of the scene has been drawn in. Look at the Mullin Memorial for example and you will see that the artist has let his imagination take over. This was a time when you could stand out in the street.

196

HIGH STREET, OMAGH.

R.3015.

High Street in a real photographic card, there are at least two shop signs for cigarettes on the left hand side. On the right hand side we have the Royal Arms Hotel and Mongomery's shop. The sign for the YMCA hangs just before Scaffe's Entry.

HIGH STREET, OMAGH. CO. TYRONE   R 5871

A similar shot taken from further up the street. On the left are McManus' shoe shop and the entrance into Bridge Street. McDermott's Chemist shop is visible at the corner of Bridge Street. On the right we have Lilliput Laundry and W J Johnston & Co. The YMCA sign is gone.

High Street, Omagh

High Street with the photographer standing in the middle of the street. The detail is not as sharp as it might have been; there is strong sunlight behind the photographer and much of the street is in shadow. You can make out the Royal Arms Hotel and Montgomery's shop but that is all.

HIGH STREET, OMAGH.

R.3007.

High Street from above the Town Hall. There is great detail in this card; you can see both the Town Hall and the Post Office clearly. Blacks Furniture shop is visible below the Post Office, they were together from about 1904 but both are now gone. Note the phone box at the Town Hall.

200